# IN THE FACE OF DARKNESS

## POEMS

by

CHRISTOPHER BIGSBY

IN THE FACE OF DARKNESS
Copyright © Christopher Bigsby, 2024

Typesetting & cover design: Natty Peterkin

ISBN 9781912665334

Christopher Bigsby has asserted his right under Section 77 of the Copyright, Designs and Patents Act 1988 to be identified as the author of this work.

All rights reserved. No part of this publication may be reproduced, stored in a retrieval system, or transmitted in any form or by any means, graphic, electronic, recorded, mechanical, or otherwise, without the prior written permission of the publisher or copyright holder.

This publication is sold subject to the condition that it shall not, by way of trade or otherwise, be lent, re-sold, hired out or otherwise circulated without the publisher's prior consent in any form of binding or cover other than that in which it is published and without a similar condition including this condition being imposed on the subsequent purchaser.

First published in 2024 by Gatehouse Press,
an imprint of Story Machine.

130 Silver Road
Norwich
NR3 4TG
United Kingdom

www.storymachines.co.uk

Set in Sabon; used under licence.

Printed and bound in the UK by 4Edge

For Allen and Rhieta Prowle

# Contents

| | |
|---|---:|
| LEE | 9 |
| THE CAMPS | 23 |
| PRELUDE | 47 |
| WAR | 55 |
| GOODBYE | 67 |
| THE WRITER AND THE ACTOR | 83 |
| JOURNEYS | 93 |
| ENDINGS | 109 |

Lee Miller was a model, a fashion photographer for *Vogue,* but, posted to London, she found herself, during the Second World War, turning to another kind of photography. Beginning with pictures of the Blitz, she followed the Normandy landings in 1944 and then proceeded across France and Germany, ending in Dachau and Buchenwald. Her photographs were never offered as art but as a record of a time, of places and people. It was her attempt to capture a version of the truth. But can a camera ever hope to do more than offer us a series of ghosts, images whose meaning slips away from us? Indeed, detached from the time and place that gave them meaning, may such images obscure rather than reveal truth? Two pictures, in particular, alarmed. In one, a concentration camp guard is seen lying dead in a ditch, yet looking oddly at peace. In another, the daughter of the Nazi Bürgermeister of Leipzig lies, like a a reclining saint, having committed suicide. Lee Miller was a photographer of complete integrity but what integrity is it that we assume to reside in a photograph, or even a poem? Can some truths never be captured in images or words?

Some of the poems that follow address the nature of war, violence, and our response to it. Others range from the personal, the fanciful, to the natural world.

# LEE

# Lee Miller

Well, Lee, there you are
Thousands of miles from what
Passes as your home and a
Million more from the world
You knew back in Poughkeepsie
Or the studio where light and
Exposure carried no threat. I see
You have traded high heels
For combat boots and care nothing
For your hair. I guess a shower
Is somewhat rare.

I have seen your room, the scotch,
Typewriter, ashtray, the books,
And in the mirror, beyond the perfume,
Your face, but of you yourself no sign,
Can you be present and absent
At the same time? Is that the secret
Of your trade?

Later, you pose, cigarette in blackened
Hand, wine bottle, jerry can, sun
In your eyes, your smile an enigmatic
Trace. Many a mile more before you
Will smile again.

No baths, either, until Munich,
In Prinzregentenplaz, where you will
Find yourself in Hitler's tub,
A photo of the Fuhrer by the
Soap dish as if he had a wish
To remind himself of who he was
When he was dressed. To your left
You will see the statue of a nude
Woman, doubtless his version of a rubber duck.

You, though, will need nothing but
Irony and the boots, your boots, at
The bath's edge, stranding to attention,
Awaiting further orders.

# Leica

She who had looked at
Calculated beauty
Young and snooty
Girls who stared
Into mirrors seeing
Nothing but their
Own perfection
Stopped
Quite
Suddenly
Turned away
Switching off
The light as if
Insight had come amidst
The lipstick and the rouge
The huge camera
Blind now, capped for the night
As she stood in the street
And felt the heat
From incendiaries
Photographing broken things
Mannequins, clothed in
Shivered glass
A public farce
As lavatories hung in space
A disgrace to those
Who lay cold and twisted
Holding nothing
But their own
Spent
Lives

She changed.
The camera she held now
Was a Leica, small and

Ready. She a fighter
In a different war
Exchanging cotton blouses
For a uniform
Trousers for a
Swirl of silk
Champagne for a
Glass of milk

In France, where she had
Once posed nude
For Man Ray
She now spent
Each day
Staring at bodies
Cracked open like
Walnuts, opening
The shutter on utter
Despair as if there
She could find a truth
Worthy of photography.

She looked where others
Turned aside,
Took pride in
Showing what the censor
Would deny.
Even so
The snow is not
Cold in her photographs
Though soldiers blow on their
Fingers and lift their
Collars high. Men do not
Die, although they lie in
Death, arms raised in
Frozen salute. The
Explosion is contained

As if there were
No danger, while
Nuns amidst the ruins
Of a church seem happy enough
As they pass by.
I hear no cry
From the child
Furniture piled high
Behind her
Alone with her thoughts
Who was once taught
Of man's divinity.
What more can she do,
Though, than raise
The camera to her eye
On days when she
Longs for nothing
More than sleep
To weep for those
She cannot save
Who gave all they had to
Give and did not live
To see the picture
She took in which
They look as if they are
Immune to danger
And free of time's
Corrosive embrace
A face whose smile
Lasts only while
You hold it in your
Hand and forget
The fate of a man
Who did not wait
For the woman
With the camera
Who smiled at him

And on a whim
Reached out a hand
To prove that he was there
As she began to doubt
A reality too hard to bear.

And so she moved on
Capturing what she could
Of a life daily more surreal
Feeling that only through
The camera lens could she
Capture men's fragile hope
Until one day, at Buchenwald,
That hope died, the camera lied,
For nothing could tell
A truth that neither eye nor mind
Would understand. Here time
Ended. The world in reverse.
No language now
But a simple curse
No music and no art
No literature
No charity, no heart,
No picture of hell
Just a tolling bell
Just a final knell.

# Ready

And so she stood at the gate
The camera loaded, film
Stretched on sprockets
Waiting for light to flood
Its darkness, black and white
And shades of grey to capture
The spectrum from blood red
To the violet of dead eyes.

She stood and waited sensing
In the air a despair with no
Correlative, no parallel, no
Paradigm, knowing, without
Seeing, seeing without
Understanding, that time
Had already stopped,
The camera's grace
No longer required

# Dachau Memorial:
# A Photograph by Lee Miller

Stare down through the freckled water
At a gentle death, reed-fringed, Millaised,
So that madness receives a grace denied by life,
And wonder at our incapacity to render truth.
There, where a willow grows aslant a brook,
He lies asleep, face mottled by reflections,
Breathing water as we once all did before we
Crawled ashore to taint the world with cruelty

No inscription is written on this water.
A date, a place, an identity of sorts
Alone can gift a necessary irony
For otherwise this is no more than a drowned man
On a September afternoon, dreaming a watery dream.
He was an SS guard at Dachau in 1945,
A bullet hole in his jacket the only mark of violence,
He is at peace, it seems, redeemed by a history of images
Which sanctify the dead and still more
Those who drift in water, stippled and fretted
By damsels, perhaps, as though nature
Took him in a justified embrace.

Truth lies not in what we see but what we know.
All that is vital to this picture we must carry there
Or mistake the image for the thing itself.
The camera blinked and what it saw preserved,
As what it did not, was not, lost therefore to the eye.
And yet Satan was beautiful and the sun did shine
As cinders rose into the sky and settled on the land.

He was born, he lived, he died, and this sullen beauty
His obituary who himself sent thousands, naked
Nameless, un-memorialised into time's unforgiving
Vortex. Other pictures than this were carried,

Like hope itself, to the furnace mouth and emptied
Into flames as agnostic as those that would lick
The faces of the dead like feral dogs driven by
Blind hunger for flesh. Only this survives so that even
Death cannot right the wrong compounded by
The camera lens and bequeathed to us his doubtful heirs.

What are we to make of this man's death we would have
Wished and, granted, celebrated? Could we see in his
Closed eyes a reflection of those we would rescue
From oblivion and if not how to justify the archive
Which preserves his form?

# Holga

She lies along a leather couch
Soft-silted with plaster dust
Shaken by the blast of bombs
Safe from moth and brittle rust

Transformed into statuary
Sanctified by death, she rests
Angelic, un-corrupt and pure
Long-fingered, mouth open for a kiss
She lies as this picture lies
A still life signifying bliss

I have seen such images before
In broken churches and on gallery walls
The virgin anguished at Christ's death
Who falters, terror struck, and falls

Yet this woman is of another breed
She walked on skulls, sucked air from
Others' lips, then laid her down to sleep
With cyanide between her teeth.
Is it for her that we should weep?

Filmed with the patina of innocence
She is preserved for us to see
Secure from justice and the silent dead
Through all eternity

# Pictures

If one took a photograph
She must have thought
Would it be possible thereby
To arrest the movement
Toward death? Would children,
Hand in hand, remain thus
Joined when time would
Separate, un-skein the wool
Of lives that might be redeemed
By so simple a device? The
Lens opens, the lens closes
And in the darkness a sensitive
Surface preserves the light which
Streams from such innocence and
Keeps it there secure against the
Agents of their undoing, the
Principals of despair. And what of
The dead? Might they re-animate,
At least regain what they had lost
At such a cost and with such pain?
And so she walked around the camp
Taking picture after picture
Storing them away against the day
They would return. And when,
At last, she understood the
Camera cannot save, did she
Consider, standing there, to join them
In the grave

# THE CAMPS

# Rabbits

At Dachau they bred Angora rabbits,
White and plump, one to a cage
The details of each inscribed on a card
Like a doctor's notes to be read
By a hospital bed

The cages, scrupulously clean, were in three tiers
Morticed, tenoned and spirit levelled
Built to last as if for a future
Denied to those who passed by
With a sigh

Their coats, proof against the winter ice,
Were smoothed by the hands of the prisoner
Who fed them four times a day.
He kept them alive
To survive

Each week he would slit the throats of a few
Skinning them with a knife he returned each night
Preparing the meat for the hungry guards
Accounting for every part
Even the heart

He, too, lived in a cage fronted with wire
In bunks three tiers high.
He was not fed four times a day
Had no coat against the cold
Never grew old

One morning two of them were dead.
At the morning parade
An officer in angora coat
Cut the man's throat.

At Dachau they bred Angora rabbits
For the officers' wives
And the officers' children
A beautiful sight
They were the purest white

# Naming

There was a man who went around the camp
And whenever he found a body stiff with death
Looked at it carefully and pronounced a name.
He tried never to repeat himself
As if each discarded corpse were newly born
And he a parent, smiling on its life-slicked face.
As the months passed, and the bodies multiplied,
You could hear his voice clear in the tainted air
Like a teacher taking register
Jacob, Esther, Rubin, Isaac, Rachel
Miriam, Saul, Sylvia, Moshe, Myron.
No one raised a hand or offered up reply
But they were present that day
Who before were absent and unknown

# Relatives

They killed not only the child
But the mother, too,
And not only her but the father,
The brother, the sister, the aunt,
The grandparents, the nephews.
They killed memory and mourning,
For there was no one left to recall
And no one left to plait a wreath.
So we must remember and mourn
Those we never knew
Inventing them to rescue
Memory and mourning, for who are we
If no one will leave a headstone,
Place a stone or invent us in our turn
And so, look, out of the mist they come.
I recognise them all. They are my mother,
My father, my brother, my sister,
My aunt, my grandparents, my nephews,
My self.

# Damsel

Double shadows
Like the chord
Of a damsel's wings
Sounding memories
Echoes of a beginning
Now ended.
Up from the water
Into air stained
Yellow with grief
Born into a
Dying light
Shedding a past
For this trembling
Moment hovering
Between now and then
Not knowing
That as they
Stand together
Hollowed by
Suffering
This is their day
To die,
Two, in the shadow
Barbed wire
Cross-stitched
And smoke
With cinders
Glowing to black

Scorched by the sun
The hum of their wings
Ceased but the song
Continued in air
Too viscous to breathe

Tomorrow they will float
On the water again
Carried by the current
That knows nothing
Of endings
Only a lover's rush
To the arms
Of the sea

## Vowels

Struck dumb and blind
He passed his fingers
Over the rough stone
And howled,
Squeezing his eyes out
Himself, fingers scooping,
Preferring jelly smear
To images that burned
His mind.
And what was speech to him
Who reached into the bran tub
And pulled out nothing
Not a syllable or consonant,
Only vowels, slide sounds
From a mouth wide
With astonishment
Drawing in air
He could not stop
Though he tried.
Here is where time ended
And with it language
The will even to shape
Form from chaos.
Sheer randomness prevailed.
This, now this, now this
And no connection
But the staccato rhythm
Of fists pounding
On flesh, that and the
Terror of a new order
Stirring darkly and
Preparing to spread
Its wings

So, out with the eyes,

Sever the tongue
Clap the ears
With cupped hands
Become a thing
For things alone
Have respite.
Yet hardly so
For here the wind
Howled round
Cold stones
And the earth
Spawned rare
Mutations. So,
All creation, then,
Sounds out vowels.
Quickly. I still hear,
Still write words
That might resuscitate.
Kill the spirit,
Break the hands
As the heart broke
Long ago.

# Re-verse

Rescind the order
Withdraw the boot
Unload the rifles
Return the loot
Empty the vehicles
Stall all the cars
Pass by the private homes
Don't raid the bars
Re-site the station
Barricade the street
Unsnatch the baby
Restore the mother's teat
Sabotage the engine
Withdraw the metal bolt
Uncouple quickly now
Un-jolt the jolt
Put down the signal lamp
Stay in the town
Derail the up train
Redirect the down
Offer them water
Give them all bread
Let them sit in comfort
Bring out the dead

Do not cross the border
Do not pass go
Do not take the high road
Do not take the low
Do not carry cases
Do not carry gold
Do not ever listen
To anything you're told
Do not disembark the train
Do not separate

Do not believe your child is safe
Do not believe in fate

Refuse the posting
Unclimb the hill
Put your clothes back on again
Refuse to kill
Undesign the building
Reroll the wire
Unpour the concrete
Damp down the fire
Separate the chemicals
Turn off the power
Open up the doors again
Don't take the shower
Don't breathe the gas in
Don't stop your heart
Don't hear the screams and cries
Don't stand apart
Don't let them go so soon
Don't wave goodbye
Don't betray their final hope
Don't let them die
Don't let them take their teeth
Don't let them burn
Don't let their ashes rise
Don't let them learn

Undo the memory
Unstitch the cloth
Unsanctify the graves
Deny the wrath
Don't accept the history
Refuse the guilt
Never trust that such a place
Was ever really built
Don't see the logic

Don't accept the pain
Don't acknowledge that such things
Could ever rise again
Untread the final steps
Retreat into the womb
Close your eyes on daylight
This your final tomb
Undo creation
Unmake the world
Destroy the atom
In which time itself was curled
Deny eternity
Annihilate space
Uninvent the error
Of the human race

Refuse the Godhead
Reject the son
Refute the power
Of three in one
Unwrite the poetry
Undo the prose
Reject the story
That the son of God arose
Unhinge the grammar
Unrhyme the verse
There is nothing words can do
To undo the curse

# Sunday Outing

In a well-pressed dirndl, white socks, sturdy shoes,
She walks precisely, glancing at a black soldier
As if meaning lay in such clear contrasts
And the world split cleanly like a log of wood.

The camp clock is at twenty past the hour
She is late or early for her rendezvous
Ordered to see if she can deny
The architecture of death and suffering.

She has no Baedeker to draw attention to finer points,
To arms and legs like narrow buttresses,
Angles and planes, shadows perpendicular,
Ovens bearing the proud maker's mark.

What will she make of the natural geography,
A hill of spectacles, a mountain of prosthetics,
Stencilled suitcases Picassoing down the stairs
In this anteroom to oblivion?

She stares at those who unaccountably live as if
Some explanation will be found on a caption underneath.
After the School of Breugel, inspired by F. Kafka.
German, artist unknown, circa 1945.

The ash from the chimneys settled on Goethe's Forest
Barely a kilometre or so away, where families,
In lederhosen spread their picnics on white cloth
Sang lieder and denied their God.

Did she see nothing, hear nothing, smell nothing
Suspect nothing, fear nothing, know nothing,
Wonder nothing, feel nothing, hope nothing,
Dream nothing, believe nothing, understand nothing,

The sun shines now on her national dress,
Catches the jewel worn so fetchingly at her neck,
Casts her shadow, more substantial and alive
Than those who struggle to believe that they survive.
We know what became of nothing

# The Market Square

There are those who say that silence
Is the only language adequate
To speak a horror beyond words,
Beyond the imagination's scope

Yet silence is a betrayal of those
On the other side of language
Ash blowing in the wind
Tumbled into eternity

And so it is that every autumn
I must stop you in this market square
Hold your arm, look into your eyes,
Offer you testament, confession, accusation

I know you would hurry on your way
Be about the business of your life
But there is something I would tell you
A story whose ending you already know

There is no meaning in this life.
I know, but listen, there is no meaning
For I have seen, I have seen, wait
There are things that must be told

It was September and I, no, just a moment more,
The leaves were, so many lives,
Like bonfires in the autumn
But we did not know, how could we know?

Please, no, I am sorry. I meant nothing
It is just that this is the point you see.
My son, he was, they took. He went.
I am alone. What can I do but this?

Do not go. I am about to tell you
About how, about what, about who.
I know I stutter. It is my only fluency.
But stay a while I beg you.

Many years ago I was taken, my child and I.
I was taken, you see. They came.
How can I explain? There are those who.
It was pain, you see, and darkness.

No, wait, wait. I am almost there
There was a place. There is a place.
There were things done, things no one.
Memories that will not. You know how it can be.

They are gone, you see, all gone,
And even those who, those others, too.
Yes, long ago, yes, that is true
But the one who did it, it was you.

No, not you yourself of course.
That is not what I meant to say at all.
The thing is. I can't begin to.
When I try to, words are like a wall

You are going, and I have not told you,
Have not explained that, wait, come back
You must hear all we suffered
You must tell me how it could be so.

And so I stand and watch a figure
Scurry darkly down a cobbled street
Then look around the market square
To see who else might have the answer.

Another autumn slowly passes.
The leaves begin to fall again

There is ash in the air
There is no end. Nobody listens.

# Silence

How do we understand
Except through words
Hammered into shape and
Bludgeoned by the past
Unless, bat-like, we send
Out our feeble squeaks
Discovering by echoes
Where we are? For Beckett
Speech was a desecration
Of silence, and there surely
Is a case for this. The very
Disproportion between
Fact and word may breed
Ironies impossible to bear.
Enormity permitted entry
Into speech becomes enormity
Sanctioned by the mouth. For
Steiner, the world of Auschwitz
Lies outside of speech, as it lies
Outside of reason. And so it does.
Words are a sea anchor dragging
Along the bottom of consciousness.
We throw them out against the
Unfathomable storm but drift
Towards the rocks of our unbeing

# One of the Thirty-Six

Precious in the sight of the Lord
Is the death of the righteous ones.
But why their death, Lord, and not their lives?
Is sacrifice the price of heavenly love?
The rabbinical fathers once wrote:
When everyone acts inhumanly
What should a man do?
He should act more humanly.
Janusz Korczak did no less.
On the last pages of his ghetto diary
Before he left, with his young charges,
For Treblinka, orphans in an age of orphans,
He wrote, I am angry with nobody,
I do not wish anybody evil.
I am unable to do so.
I do not know how one can do it.
We know. He did not. That is what made him
A righteous man.
At Treblinka, there is a rock
On which is written his name,
Janusz Korczak (Henryk Goldszmit).
He travelled, you understand, incognito,
As do all the righteous,
One of the thirty-six,
Not justifying man in the eyes of God
But justifying God
In the eyes of man.

# Paris in the Snow

La syphilis est curable
Said the notice in the pissoir,
Its metal curved like the
Broken spiral of a shell.
If so, it was the only thing
That was that winter when the snow
Could not conceal the splintered
Wounds of war and every street
Was lit by candles that marked
A death

Through the fog, beyond the man
With an umbrella and the dark nudes
Of the Palais de Chaillot,
The Eiffel Tower rose like a
Memory, its brash lattice a creature,
Neck craning, four legs planted in
The ice

In the Jardin des Tuileries are
Stacked chairs clustered around
Bare trees shorn of leaves like the
Women whose hair is cut at the
Roadside because they have let love
Undo them, allowed hate to fall
Silently with their clothes on
Cold floors

A city occupied is a musical hall
That echoes with nothing, a song
With no applause, and yet it smiles
Brightly. Its familiar sights now
Prostitute themselves for the
Conqueror, sleeping with the enemy
Then waking at dawn, haggard with

Regret. Ah, the curve of the Odeon,
The uplift of Montmartre, the winking
Of street lamps, the warm pulse of the
Sacre Coeur, all surrendering to the
Seducer's art.

# Roadside Burial

The troops wear white
Like brides, as they march
In the snow, as they go
Through trees like tall
Sentries, moving from one
Place to another, brothers
Out for a stroll. They have
No role but to march and fight
For right, they were told,
For freedom, a whole dictionary
Of words they have heard
Breath steaming in cold air,
Feeling despair as they pass
A freshly dug grave. No wave
From the chaplain, head bowed,
Helmet like a toadstool cap,
Looking into dark earth that
Gives birth to nothing but a man
Staring into a sky he cannot see,
His eyes closed for eternity,
Dead by calculation or mere
Chance on this forgotten road
In a forgotten France.

# PRELUDE

# Which?

A premeditated birth, they said,
Demonic calculation. To so ingest,
De-seminate a man who thereby
Is confederate to evil. Luciferic
Conception. To erect placental
Barrier against true justice,
Refuse the honest price of
Witch's trade. Take her away and
Let her swell with breeding and
When the bitch deflates, then let her hang.

And yet there was a mystery to those
Whose lives became their only grace,
Flared into sudden beauty then
Blackened into night. Supple with
Acceptance, tensile with revolt,
Accomplices to anonymity, they
Stumbled on a meaning they had
Mislaid, like a wedding ring
Concealed in rags which shines
A second in the flames. And so
They died with fingers burned
But wedded once again to truth.

And with their deaths we break a
Dark conspiracy! There's lessons
Here for those with eyes to see!

And so there are, but no one here
Can catechise a faith so late
Discovered and so totally displayed.
They hang from silken threads
Who now can summon up the dead.

# Elvira

In 1563, in Toledo, Elvira, young, pregnant,
Christian, was tortured on report
Of her dislike of pork, and habit
Of changing her underclothes each week,
Sure signs of secret Jewry.
Urged to confess, she explained
That the meat made her stomach turn
While she had been taught to practice cleanliness.
They knew liars, though, and had a way with them.
Stripped naked, she was raised up with ropes
And tortured by priests until at last,
Close to death, she confessed everything.
Mercifully, she lost only her baby, her property,
Use of her body and her sanity.
She was redeemed, they said,
Only her soul was dead.

# The Last Warrior

She is tired
Of losing what there is
To lose

She is waiting
For an end
To time

She is looking
For signs that have long
Since gone

She is alone
At the end of
A line

She is dreaming
Of eyes the colour
Of milk

She is searching
For somewhere
To hide

She is hearing
The echo of
Distant drums

She is singing
For those who
Have died

She is remembering
Those who have
Gone before

She is hoping
That time
Will end

She is dying
For loss of her own
True tribe

She is desperate
For want of
A friend

She is telling
A tale she has
Told before

She is listing
The nations
Of men

She is hoping
For hope to depart
At last

She is sure
She will not
Know when

She is motionless
Now in the
Timeless dust

She is flying
With the spear that
Is hurled

She is fading
Along with the
Setting sun
She is one
With the
Spirit world

# WAR

# Dresden

They bombed Dresden on Valentine's Day.
From a secret admirer, a holocaust. The flares
They dropped were called Christmas trees,
Frozen lights on a not so silent night

The city pulled darkness around it like a cloak
Lights, give me lights, and lights we supplied
Blossoming red and yellow in the puddled streets
A garden of fire blistering the skin of the city
Curling it back to its medieval core, a shrivelled
Cinder of time, Pompei shadowed and inert

And in the cellars, baked like bread, with
Dough fingers, crisp crusted, blackened,
Splayed in supplication, lay neat rows
Of those who offered their breath to feed
The fire that consumed them and licked
The casements and vaulted roofs that
Sheltered nothing but a broken piety

For day on day they gnawed on the bones
Of a city whose carcass lay streaked with
Blood, picked over by circling birds of prey
Black shadows in a liquid sky, their droppings
Burying the world and the world's hope

Men and women ignited in the street,
So many matches struck on the rough edge of
Disregard. Charcoaled in an instant, at
One thousand degrees, the fluids in their bodies
Evaporated so that they remained wholly
Recognisable, though carbonised, revenge as sweet
As the smell that lingers a week, a month,
A life, a memory of heat

# Burial

At Omaha beach, where men died
As easily as breathed and the
Air was full of blood that
Clotted in the eyes, and sand
Was turned to glass, a man fell
And in falling reached out for
What was not there, his arm a
Memory, deaf, too, for he never
Heard his scream but woke to a man
Who took his pain away. Later he was
In a hospital, a row of tents
Seeded in a field, a high yield
Crop, and here they probed and cut
And sewed, then sent him on his way to
Saint Laurent-sur-Mer where he was
Stacked with others, twelve to a side and
Leaking a little blood, on a plane that
Flew into the setting sun while far way
A woman waited for a man who has two
Graves, one where a plane flew from
A darkening sky, and one where an arm
Slowly drifted on a strengthening tide.

# Vietnam

She runs towards us, arms outstretched
Skin hanging down, the faded flags
Of a long past war, her mouth sounding
A scream we may not hear but feel
Reverberate louder by far than the
Explosions which belly forth
Behind her in the paddy fields. Her
Face contorted with pain, her body
No longer flesh and blood, but a symbol
A sign, a hieroglyph inscribed for the
World to read, an accusation levelled
At those who came to win hearts and minds
And lost more than fifty thousand dead
Along with those they forbore to count
Except that a pair of ears and a simple
Long division would please the Senators
Who believed that wars like these were
Simply won and the cost easy to bear

Today, she still lives and though she
Carries the scars, and feels a pain or two,
Few photographers now seek her out
Or send her picture around the world.
Indeed, there is some embarrassment
She survived at all and thus does
Damage to an image so much more real
Than her for how could she walk and smile,
Cook eggs and catch the bus to work.
She does not understand she owes us
So much more than the banality of her
Daily life. She rose in flames, was our
Phoenix, our Joan of Arc, how, then,
Could she be allowed to slake her thirst,
Shade herself against the heat, and let
Her shadow go, when once she was

Flooded with true significance.

# The IRA Has Accepted Responsibility

Sudden light. No more.
Thought. Being. Bleached.
Evacuated of everything
Leaving
Nothing

Images. Something far off
Then nothing but a memory
Of light
Extinguished

Blank blank blank
Shape shapes shape
Blank. What?

Sound first. Floating, uncertain
A dog somewhere, perhaps,
Distant as a
Memory
Undone

Then sleep, or some such,
Dreams
Sound again
Regular
A wheezing
Asthmatic
Breathing

Then light reborn
Ceiling edged with
Sun-bright circles
Curtain rings

Everything broken

Nothing belonging
With anything else
At all

Rubber on rubber
Sigh of a trolley's wheels perhaps
A bed, yes a bed
And tubes and
A pain somewhere

Me, walking down a road
With something I must do

The light, or memory of light,
And the picture rising up
As I sink down

Someone at my side
Now, not then,
This new now
Hollowed out of time

Awake, she asks, are you
Awake? Her face swims,
Swims slowly out of
View

Are you alright?
Can you hear me
Nurse, could he be
Deaf?

And all it was, of course,
Was a bomb
Designed to change
Someone's mind

And I no more than a way
Of asking the question
More
Forcefully

An arm, a leg, they tell me
At last, looking down smiling
Brightly

It could have been
So much worse
You might have been killed
You know

Today I can feed myself
And even stroll
For a while with very little
Pain

And all for walking
Down the street
For a reason I no longer
Recall

# The News

The television news is discrete
About the effects of Semtex
On the human body.
We are shown buildings
Spilled across the street
The broken ribs
Of shattered timber,
Windows blinded by the blast
Dark liquids flowing
In the shadowed gutter.
But the dead are so many
Smiling faces, school photos
Wedding snaps, people laughing
In the sun as if the bomb had left
Them quite intact only the
Tense of their lives changed.
What, then, were they shovelling
Into those plastic bags?
What was hanging down before they
Flipped it in? And what are the firemen
Hosing away? A warning was received
But the details were imprecise
So that running away from death
They found it, where others had left it
Relying on the discretion of the
Television news to reassure us that
Death is no more than switching off
The light at the end of the day
Or watching the screen as a bright spot
Fades to a phosphor glow.
There are truths, it seems,
Too disturbing for us to know

# GOODBYE

# Too Late

She lay
Where she had lain
All day
Concealed only by
A curtain
From those
Who would go home
Soon, who suffered
From a broken arm
Asthma, loneliness
And when she refused
To draw another breath
They accepted her decision

I was too late
To hear
The breath
Not taken
Still warm
To the touch
She had gone.
I knew that
I kissed absence.

When the chaplain
Summoned by my sister
Offered his unctuous
Unction, his bleeper
Sounded in the middle
Of the Lord's Prayer
As if God had detected
An error and wished
To correct him.
He, and we, pretended
It was mute but eventually

He checked it to see if
Another soul was calling
Him more urgently

She had left
Before I arrived
Her journey and mine
Did not intersect
As yet.

Why, in a million years,
Have we not found
The words to say
What it is to lose
What cannot be lost?

We keep a Thesaurus
Of empty language
Secure in the faith
That the very hollowness
Is a mark of true
Sincerity.
There is a reason
For cliches, for language
Uniquely disinterred
To mark our
Incapacity to express
True feeling.
Just as love
Is a word that falls
Far short of its
True meaning
So condolences
Bereavement
Loss
Loved ones
So sorry

Do nothing more
Than confess
That we meet
Somewhere
Words
Cannot
Go

Do I betray, then,
In alchemising pain
Into words on a page?
Is there treachery
In voiding privacy,
In revisiting
The moment
The clock
Stopped?
Four minutes
Past three, they said,
As if to remind me
I was too late, that I lived in time
And she did not,
That for her the tick
Tock of life
Had ceased
While for me
The sand
Still sifted
Down
Grain
By
Grain
Pain
By Pain

For a living pulse
I substitute

Broken
Verse
As though thereby
To breathe life
Where no breath
Misted
The cold
Eyeball
Of the
Death
Watcher

This is the
Goodbye
I never uttered
This is me
Lifting the curtain
Just in time.
Here I am
To tell you
What I never
Did,
The child's lament
I
Loved
You
And
Never
Told
You
So.

# Internment

We walked from the lychgate,
The undertakers' men
Shuffling like a centipede
Professionally solemn
While we, the amateurs,
Followed on behind
Learning by doing,
Actors trying not to act
True feeling and propriety
In uncertain harmony

They led us past the graves
Of those who had themselves
Shuffled off this world
Graves aslant, lichen stained
Words telling us what
We would not know
That beginnings contain
Endings, that there is
No reprieve. Much loved
Mother, father, son, daughter,
Their graves no longer tended
In a quiet churchyard where time
One distant day reached its end

We were too few
To sing the songs we knew
Too many to claim the privacy
We craved. There, where my own
Birth was inscribed, and memories
Were stirred, my mother was
Summoned unto God, sung to her
Rest by a boy whose voice was
Sound turned into light

Then to the cheap theatrics of the
Crematorium with its perfunctory
Prayers, synthetic tunes and velvet
Curtain gliding, oh so reverently,
On silent motors as if you might expect
The departed to appear once more
To take a bow

Then on into the air
With two more funerals ahead
And one behind with other strangers
Shedding tears for other years
Come to nothing

And then the drive back like a family
When the bride has left laughing, even,
Remembering, but ultimately bereft
The ceremony complete we claim her
Back from those who carried her
Those who committed her
Those who burned the past.
For now she is ours again
At last

# Funeral Feast

Afterwards
In the house where I was raised
We meet again
To talk away
The pain
These the voices
These the names
Recalled on
Christmas presents
Long ago
Postal orders
Handkerchiefs and pens
Crystal sets that stayed
Mute sending messages
To those ill-equipped
To hear

These are cousins
I have not seen
For thirty years
Or more
Brought to this place
By someone who is
No longer here.
And so we laugh
And talk
Kiss, wave,
And say goodbye
While somewhere
Flames consume
Not my mother
But all that remains
Of a past which once
Seemed all there
Could ever be

# House Clearance

We looked through the cupboards,
Opened all the drawers,
Blankly looking for something
That would speak to us
As she had done before we knew
How precious words could be.
Who would have thought
That neatly folded clothes,
Corners squared away,
Would have the power to move
By their simple geometry.
And in a box
School medals and certificates,
To me no more than trinkets
From a forgotten past,
To her so many treasures stored away,
Memories of what once was
But would be no more.
And further back her ballet shoes
From a time I never knew
When she tulipped her arms
Above her head and danced across the stage
Who at the end could hardly walk at all,
She who once floated like a breeze,
Shaped the air through which she moved,
Lived a poetry that slipped away
When family, war and time
Destroyed the grace she lived.
Was her life no more
Than a gathering of scraps,
Once radiant with meaning,
Now so many autumn leaves
Drifting silently down
To be swept so casually away.
The walls are bare, furniture sold

Or given to those for whom
This place, this person, has no past.
Soon, the house, where laughter
Once echoed, will itself
Be
Gone.
And where, then, will I hang
My memories
When there are
No more walls
And the windows
Are
All
Blind?

# The Photo on the Wall

I grew up with a photo on the wall.
You are just like him, my mother said,
Except he was dead in the war.
But what could that mean to me
Who never called him uncle
And thought Percy a name too
Soft to claim as kin. Eternally
Smiling and uniformed, he was
Shot down the day his son was born.
He carried the news over Holland
In his Halifax, death in its belly,
Death in the Perspex turret like a
Lizard's eye, flicking left and right
In search of prey, death in the fire
That shone that night as his child lost
What it never knew, a father's love,
And my mother's memories like a flower
Pressed in a book. To me he was hardly
Worth a moment's thought as I followed
My own pathfinder on a still bright night
But even I noticed, from time to time,
As my mother's eyes strayed to the
Photo on the wall to recall a lost life
A lost friend, a lost youth, a lost family.
There are other photographs of Percy,
Pictures of him as a chorister in the Abbey
And playing in the snow of Canada
But it is this one that framed my youth
And defined the pain my mother felt
And which it took me a lifetime to
Understand. For when she, in turn, died,
He became real at last, smiling that it took me
So long to feel another's pain.

# All Dreams Are Memories

It was in November, when the first frost
Brittled the grass and the sun arced low
Across the sky, that another leaf fell
Ungently from the tree. My sister,
Who had summoned the chaplain,
In the hospital and celebrated our mother's
Life, in a grey church lit only by the
Silver of a young boy's voice, surrendered
To a dark flower which bloomed unseen
In her lungs, her spine, her brain at last.
The lights were turned off one by one
As she left the room and closed the door
On a life as full of miracles as all lives are

She lay those last days, too long, too short,
Her mind swimming through seas of memories
Distorted, like a stick in water, by the steady
Pulse of drugs. There was a horse, she said,
Her voice a whisper, eyes intense, and a donkey.
It's the morphine, said the nurse, but I knew
There was a horse, one winter, pulling a milk cart.
It slipped on ice, bottles tumbling like white painted
Indian clubs. Legs broken, eyes wide, it stained
The snow nicotine with a spray of piss, deep crimson
With arterial blood. No donkey, though. It came from
Another time and place retrieved as she set out
On a road she had never travelled before
And by her side her daughter, who watched and held
Her hand as if she had slipped overboard and could be
Rescued still from the ocean cold.

She was a time traveller
Who had bent a blade of grass
Breathed in the common air
And changed the world she touched

Beckoning us forward now,
Not knowing where she journeyed
Or why but making of her life
A milestone for us who follow.

Each death is a loss to all
Each life a gain.
Her footprints
Are still
Fresh upon
The sand

She bequeathed us
A central truth.
Like summer squirrels,
We bury moments
Against a coming winter.
There was a horse,
You see.
All dreams
Are memories
All memories
Are dreams

# THE WRITER AND THE ACTOR

# For Delmore Schwartz

The slender reach of a despairing arm
Was never enough for him. The inrush
Of feeling pressed against other nerves
Than those responsive to surrender.

Words were a far country, a distant prospect
Which impelled him past those who watched
And trailed a sombre affection across his path
Leaving a glistening film of commitment
He found too easy to evade.

As he sat in the Chelsea, bottle by his side,
The iron radiators too hot to touch,
Oblivious to the snow blown through the window,
Like a scalpel drawn across the grey flesh
Of a cadaver, he cut a bloodless line
Whose slow erupting flesh contained no seed.

Changeless in inconstancy, the single note
To sound beneath the chatter of communion
Unblessed was silent to those whose ears
Were tuned to something other than the
Anguished cry of self-pity alchemised to art.

He died, not from a surfeit of the real
But from suffocation, a dense compacted crowd
Of conspiring souls clotting the arteries.
I'm guilty, he cried, punish me, punish me.

And so they did, in his mind, with a disregard
Which bleached the blood at source
And left him stranded, Moby Dick on a flat,
White beach, or a single bird sucked
Into the day's eye and the aphasia
His life was squandered to escape.

He never merited the one forgiveness he needed
Above all, the only absolution he would recognise.
In dreams begin responsibilities, in the mind's domain
The quiet grace which can never render peace
Except through reflection in the dark pupil

Of another eye, the budding iris of the friend
Whose solace he could only see as envy.
All he could do was etch the smallest
Scratch on the eye's lens, inscribe his need,
Delineate his reckless hope, so that he would
Always see the world framed by his disdain,
Marked by the passing irony of a maker
Made to unmake the real and offer us
The residue.

Who would have thought The Velvet Underground
And U2 would hear an echo, that Berryman
And Bukowski would celebrate a man
Dead at fifty-two in the Chelsea and made to duel with
Bellow even from the grave.

# Joseph Brodsky

So, Joseph Brodsky imagined into being by
His parents' desire to free themselves in time.
Before the foetal heart could beat they saw
A shadow slip between the bars, the shadow
Of a hand that reached beyond, two plotters
Planning against the day a child of theirs
Would sound against the State's oblivion
And find a voice to speak their lives
With total clarity.

And so
They made
Love
Where no love
Was before

Somewhere, in the womb, freedom multiplies
Its cells so that, one day, the poet speaks
And his parents live again, free at last

# The Dance and Not the Dancer

There is no warrant for hysteria.
Grace is not born out of suffering,
Delivered by some midwife priest of language.
Do not drive the car with one finger
Balanced against temptation.
Too many poets have plunged through
The gaps in reality, my friend,
A smear of words all that survived the accident.
Do not, I pray you, listen to those who say
All we require is that you should offer up
A thin biopsy, like a curled shaving
From a pencil, a cuticle of self
To be inspected for pathology.
It is the words that give the reason why
Not you who scrawl them on the sky.

# Tonight at the Royal Court

An actor trails in from formica digs
In Clapham, clutching divorce papers in a
File from Paper Chase to motivate him in a
Murder he must commit, not once but twice
This being Thursday, and with no more than a
Crunchy Bar to press him to the deed

In his hand he clutches a Methuen play text
Now heavily annotated where the author and
Director have argued themselves to stasis
In the theatre bar. After two months, he is
Royal Courted out.

Admired by Time Out and The Guardian
Despised by the Standard, deplored by
The Telegraph and ignored by England
North of Barnet, he has nothing more
In store than a casualty in Casualty
Or a body in The Bill

Yet, for an hour or so, he will step into
The light and allow that light its alchemy
Transforming space into place, bending time,
Fracturing the self into a kaleidoscope of
Selves, to the basso profundo of the tube.

Here, where the day is blinded,
And to the rustle of the After Eights,
He sings his song and cries his tears
Before sailing south to Battersea and
Clapham where the laundromats tumble,
Takeaways scatter their confetti in the street,
And dead souls await the kiss of Dionysus
Before once more seeking out
The light of all our dreams.

Was it for this he once imitated a tree
Exercised his voice and body
Planned an acceptance speech?
What is he but a voice sounding in the dark
A body inscribing its needs
A soul in search of meaning
And what is this except acceptance?

# Lear

Fall and cease to the
Sound of howl at
Death unfathomable
Beyond all bearing.
Nothing come to
This, breeding a
Sharp meaning for
One such as he who
Divided himself for
Love of himself and
Was divided in turn
Flesh from his rib
A forked Adam with
No cliff high enough
To dash his guilty
Brains, no wisdom
Sufficient to justify the
Sacrifice of what was
Not his to lose. Why
Should a dog, a horse,
A rat have life, he
Asked, and thou no
Breath at all? Because,
Old Lear, you never
Asked them if they
Loved you.

# JOURNEYS

# Eden

Beyond the funereal ribbon of the road
From Basra to Baghdad is Eden, kempt
Contained, unsubtle as a prophecy,
Its small brown fruit shrivelled in the sun.
And should there be those who doubt
The true location of our innocence
A metal plate obligingly authenticates
This paradise now fenced around
Against those who would re-enter it.

There, on the elbow of two rivers,
Tigris and Euphrates, where the waters
Braid like copulating snakes,
And the double surge mounts up tumescent,
Lies a broken deer, its neck inclined,
One eye a silver mirror, the other
A frosted grape. Half in water
Half still rooted in the land, coiled for
The leap, retrained by calculating hand.
And as the waves pulse coldly on the shore
So, grey intestines throb with life once more.
The mouth still drinks, the fur floats free.
In Eden's shade, a mystery.

# Journey

I wake to find us underway
To feel the rhythm and the sway
To see a world of flesh and bone
To speak the words I've never known

New-born lambs and rutting sows
Rictus horses, mottled cows
Stationary in flying field
With stubble burn across the wield

Upper lip of graceful bridge
Sharp-edged scarp of sabre ridge
Valley's cleft and distant haze
Passing visions, passing days

White-planked mill and circled straw
Flooded fields and purple tor
Rape seed yellow, clover green
Things imagined, things half seen

Foil of river, furl of sea
What can these things mean to me
Sudden ponds and dark-tilled soil
Rising birds form silver coil

Hover hawk and page-white swan
Young child waving, young child gone
Speed is rising ever yet
Interest on a growing debt

Images begin to blur
Leaf and water, feather, fur
Shadows running faster still
Over brook and swelling hill

Mind is racing, heart on fire
Rustic cottage, broken byre
Life is now at fullest flood
Hear the beating of the blood

Flying in the noonday sun
Now the race is almost done
Rabbit warren, wild cat's lair
Cemetery and village fair

See them rush away from me
Future turned to history
Cornflowers, oats and barley field
Now I know my fate is sealed

Then I feel momentum slack
Easing screws within a rack
Once again the pulse of time
Re-establishes the rhyme

Sewage clocks and silo tower
What the minute, what the hour
Poplar sentries, willow tear
Absence of a startled deer

Sheep in panic, wild hare jump
Stain of poppies, garbage dump
This way, that way, somewhere go
Suddenly I feel it slow

Far ahead a dying sun
Journey's end is journey done
Life is stilling, here the end
Gathered darkness at the bend

Rhythm is broken, metre lost
What the purpose, what the cost?

I no longer understand
Hieroglyph of lake and land

So it stops, the evening come
Eye is dim and voice is dumb
A single light shines far away
To mock the thought of parted day

Out of time and out of reach
The only sound a barn owl's screech
As feathers fold the dark is still
The perfect place for it to kill

A mouse's heart is torn away
To feed a hunger for the day
To open eyes now fisted tight
To end the waiting, end the night

In moor and forest, crag and glen
Badger's set and fox's den
A smear of life encrusts the earth
Conspires to bring about my birth

Future blank and memory ceased
A distant glow corrupts the east
With blood-licked lambs and spittled fawn
The birthing skin is slowly torn

The voyage begins, I feel it start,
The cord of death begins to part
An inescapable refrain
Sets me to tread the world again

I wake to find us underway
To feel the rhythm and the sway
To see a world of flesh and bone
To speak the words I've never known

# The Door

Kock, knock
Here is the door
Nothing stirs
I am a stranger
Travelled many miles
I ask for comfort
And perhaps a smile
The wind howls
The snow drives down
I would be content
With a curse or a frown
But no one replies

Knock, knock
Here is the door
Beyond it lies
Light and warmth
Music and food
The one that I wooed
In the time of my youth

Knock, knock
Is there no one within
Who will let me in
The night is cold
I have travelled far
I followed a star
I searched for a place
I knew before
I come to this door
Who have known disgrace
I look for a face
And a dress of lace

Knock, knock

My shield is broken
There is rust on my sword
I never found
The treasure hoard
I never killed
The dangerous dragon
But lost myself
In an earthenware flagon
Unworthy man
I confess that I am

Knock, knock
And then at last
The door stands wide
I smell corruption
On every side
There is death within
This sacred place
A truth that is more
Than I can face
I deserted them all
Through the sin of pride
For I am the one
Who needlessly lied
I followed my fortune
And searched for my fate
But have come at last
To this fortress gate
A place so dear
For my children are here

Knock, knock
Goes the sound
Of my heart
With a sudden start
A cloying fear
Grips the heart of me

For what do I see
But the bones
Of the dead
And the fearful head
Of the dragon I sought
I look at the ruin
That I have brought
The treasure I lost
At terrible cost
I need never
Have left
For the point
Of my quest
Without a rest
Lay behind the door
Now covered in gore
That I closed the day
I went away
Wife and children
Children and wife
They were the grail
Of my pitiful life

Now there is nothing
For me to do
But bury the dead
And sprinkle the rue
I hear the sound
Of coffin nails
As I place the family
That I have found
Deep in the ground
I can never restore
What I had before
The love of a woman
The love of a child
Meek and mild

Yet strong as steel
With the power to heal
A restless heart
And now I must start
As I did before
Close the door
On this awful sight
Submit myself
To deepening night
Leave this place
Forget the face
Of the woman I knew
And the precious few
Who had watched me go
All that time ago
And waited each day
For my return
As the fields
Were burned
But I never came
I carry the blame

Knock, knock
I close the door
As it was before
And climb the hill
Who never did kill
The dragon who slayed
My wife one day
For I was far away.
I should have known
Though I might roam
That what I sought
Could not be caught
For it lay behind me
In my home.

I throw a rope
Bereft of hope
Over the branch
Of a sycamore tree
Woe is me
The other end
Is around my neck
At break of day
The birds will peck
Eyes that have seen
What they would not see
So now I hang
In the still of night
And think of my life
And my dearest wife.

Knock, knock
Go the heels
Of my shoes
As I rise up high
And my spirit flies
To the distant hall
I knock on the door
And hear the call
Of those in coffins
Beneath the ground
The terrible sound
Of a nether world
Where I myself
Will now be hurled.

Knock, knock
I open the door
To a terrible roar
Of sulphur and flames
And the Devil reclaims
A suffering soul

As the Bible foretold
I cannot believe
What it is I am seeing
The fearful face
Of an awful being
A scarlet head
A thrashing tail
I fall on my knees
And begin to quail
He opens his mouth
To announce my doom
When a woman in white
Enters the room
He turns around
Stamps on the ground
With a frightening leer
But shaking with fear
For an angel is here
And never so dear
For to save my life
Comes my beautiful wife
She lifts me up
And raises a cup
To my aching lips
And even as I
Begin to sip
We are flying high
In cerulean sky
Until we come
To a heavenly gate
It is never too late
To change your fate.

Knock, knock
The door flies wide
We step inside
My aging wife

Now a youthful bride
The voice sounds clear
"Who is this comes here?"
"It is I, my Lord,
Who once tied the cord
With a husband dear
Who is with me here."
"You may enter in
One without sin. But what of him?"
"He is one, my Lord,
Who went abroad
In search of a treasure
Beyond all measure
And forgot for a while
That a simple smile
Is worth more than gold
That to have and to hold
Is the essence of life
That and the love
Of a dutiful wife.
But now I believe
He will understand
And hold my hand
Be faithful and true
And in awe of you
Who forgives us all
Whenever we fall."
For one last time
The voice spoke clear
"You may enter in
And have no fear
Your love is strong
It negates all wrong
You both are one
Your race is run
I grant release
And eternal peace."

And at this word
A single bird
Began to fly
Through gates closing tight
In a graceful flight
To the earth below
Where in driving snow
A stranger saw
A fastened door
And began to strike
With all his might

Knock, knock
I am a stranger
Travelled many miles
I ask for comfort
And perhaps a smile

The door opened wide
And just inside
Stood the woman I loved
With a turtle dove
And two children besides.
This is now
Where I abide.
I found the treasure
Beyond all measure
I slew the dragon
That was in my heart
We are never apart.
And on winter nights
When the stars are bright
I opens the door
That was closed before
For who can know
In the driving snow
If a desperate man

May be passing by
Looking for love
In a woman's eye.

# ENDINGS

# When?

When do we cross the line
From autumn into winter?
When does youth become age,
Hope despair, true love
Indifference, a playground
Game set aside upon a whim?
One day time's ambush paints
A mottled mark upon the skin,
Blind Pew's black spot. As the
Hands of a silent clock move on,
The eye's clarity begins to fade,
Like the beauty of a maid.
So, too, the flower whose petals
Close too slowly so that a sliver
Of ice cuts directly to the heart.
For frost will come, snow will
Have its day. December follows May.

# Snowdrops

What is to be said for
The false promises of
Snowdrops? With the worst
Of winter still to come
They curtsey, bending their
Heads demurely as if
Civility were enough,
As the sleet beats on the
Church door like men
In search of sanctuary
Or the life of a priest,
Surplus flying white.
Why are they here
So early when the sun
Sleeps in rather than
Rise and face a wind
That turns feathers into
A ruff and blows the stuff
Of autumn against the
Legs of those who slide
On the black slick of
Streets polished to a
Sheen? Still they curtsey,
Green young women,
With white bonnets
Nodding together in
Assent to some principle
That all the world denies,
Telling, with their slender
Beauty, January lies.

# Butterfly

As the butterfly flutters
On the window with the sound
Of a pen on paper, a rough hand
Brushing over silk, the patina
Of her wings falls a shattered
Rainbow ground to dust
Until the stained glass beauty
Of a frenetic life is surrendered
And down she tumbles sycamoring
Through tangled webs, dry saliva
Threads spun those months ago
When life was fresh and all were
Hungry for the day that now ends
With a dying butterfly among the
Mud of autumn, fanning memories
As a breeze stirs and she rises
One last time, ever higher, on
Dead wings whose spectrum shines
The promised fire, cold now,
Its colours brittle as ice

# The Gardener

A rabbit lies
Slick with dew
As if just delivered
From the womb,
In thrall to
Falling, eyes a
Liquid white
As maggots feed
In a frenzy of
Blind desire.
The gardener
Dead heads flowers
With a casual
Fluency, tears
Plants from still
Warm earth and
Lights a pyre
Where he burns
Those whose
Sudden beauty is
Now faded.
The time of
Their time is
Done. The sun
Is set on the
Yellowed bee and
The lavender flower
The crimson rose
And the twilight hour

# The Closing Down Sale

Flies pick their way blindly
On the carpet pile as though
The air is too thick for wings
To support. Or they are
cataracted in muslin shrouds,
Turned by a spider like a
Roasted lamb over a burning pit.

Wasps, settle themselves in
Sugar-coated plums, drunk on
Fermented sweetness, death
Just a frost away, stinging, still,
The hand that reaches through
As if in memory of what they were
Before alcohol took their wits away.

A line of snail tracks, shining flakes
Of mica, are baked by a sun which
Slants ever lower, dipping beneath
The trees, shadows a little closer to the
House each day. Smoke hangs in the air
As if ready to retreat into the ashes
That glow vermilion in the fading light.

Crows splinter in the flesh of the corn
Or, rising, mourners in the evening sky.
Along the telephone wires starlings
Gather like notes on a stave, ready to
Play us into autumn this September day.

On the tree, apples, tribal scars pecked
By nodding jays in formal suits
Fluttering for balance then shivering
Through the branches to rise into a sky
Whose blue already seems a memory.

Beech leaves, like gold flakes from
A temple in the jungle, yesterday's faith,
Drift down in knowledge of the Resurrection.
Berries swell and tighten, red and black,
The one sweet and welcoming,
The other with poison for the blood
Or power to stir love in a spinster's
Heart even with winter's promise on the wind.

Swans with grey signets leave the river
To preen themselves, old ladies waddling
Home from shopping and squatting to sleep
In a sun blurred by the thinnest cloud.

Moor hens, heads jerking like sand dancers
Performing for a theatre queue, their mouths
Forced open by apples strut back to the
River where their chicks have flown
Or the fox, whose dark tracks betray its habits,
Licks its grinning lips, the chick's education
Coming too late in a fading day.

And though they must know that death stalks
Close at hand, rabbits, fear dulled by a
Summer's habit, scuff the silted soil of burrows
Which scar the lawn and nuzzle grass
That mercifully has ceased to grow
So the mower can be returned to the shed
To rust a little in the months ahead.

Squirrels flow their lazy patterns through the
branches, clutching stolen hazel nuts
A memory of summer for winter days,
So many children playing Battleships with x
Marking the spot. They read the future,
Guard against tomorrow even as the mayfly
Dies on the wing with few regrets, having

No intimation of life's brevity, believing
Eternity to be contained within the day
While death is but a wing's beat away.

The moles seem to have given up
Their blind rushing in the dark
Like underground trains buffeting
From side to side. No fresh soil
Appears, no heaving of the grass
Where they pass, just dry earth
And a scatter of stones,
So many bones on a desert sand.

Horse chestnuts, leaves tinged brown,
Fruit prickling outward, bravely brace
For the sticks of impatient boys eager
To break their mahogany hearts.
The maple turns from orange to bronze
To crimson tinged with black, opting
For funeral wear as the sun withdraws its love
And a dove wonders why it is solitary
In the sky even as the river that flows
At the garden's edge, its brittle sparkle
Dulled, bottle green and slate grey,
Slides on its way waiting for winter rain
To swell it again so it may flood the
Tunnels of the departed moles, sink
Liquid roots into rabbit holes, the
Warm retreats of farmyard mice
Transforming pitted stubble fields
Into the smoothest mirrors of ice.

The reed cutter has passed this way
Slicing through the silver eye of the
Stream, hooking weeds, his crooked finger
Bent by the water, beckoning the maiden's
Hair drifting like thought this way and that

With the slow speed of a child's day
And of a childhood lost.

High above, the geese begin to shape
Themselves, to drive a wedge into the sky
Breaking open their tomorrow with the
Arrow they will follow and in following
Become the sign they form.

This, then, is the world about to change,
Thistle-tufted, dry-leaved, wind-tumbled,
A moment when ripeness meets decay
The seesaw tilts, the ball hangs in the air,
And love feels its first regret,
September, when the smell of earth
Recalls the planting and the harvest time
Beginning and end both still in sight
Until at last the day's dominion is
Surrendered to the sad democracy of night.

This is the closing down sale
A time for stock taking
Everything must go and so,
In one last spasm of energy,
They all appear, side by side,
Rabbit and squirrel, swan and jay,
Knowing that this is the final day
With falling leaves and cankered rose
Aware that a door is about to close
That now is the final time to buy,
And for some at least the time to die.

As for me, I am where I have
Always been. Come and find me
So I will know where I am, that I am,
For I, too, see the sky darken
Feel the temperature begin to fall

No longer hear the night owl's call.
And with the first winter frost
Will remember only what I have lost.

# North Norfolk

Samphire fringed, seal slicked and black,
The salt marsh frays to salt sea edge
Its summer plenitude now turned to lack
With frozen birds in calcined sedge

Frost-brittled, ice sheeted, the colonnaded reeds
Jostle and chafe as housewives at a sale
While in the tufted grass and sullen weeds
Lie flattened frogs and broken snails

The sky is stained a sickly yellow
As if a malady breathed through the land
A stranded bull begins to bellow
Straying from pasture to pitted sand

Seals, slug-like, shudder and ripple as they lurch
Across the sighing shingle to the surf
While, high above, the stunted finger of a church,
Flint-mottled houses that once spoke a merchant's worth

Every decade the sea reclaims the marsh
Spreading like blood from a broken skull
Life in this kingdom is testing and harsh
Like the shriek from the sky of a dying gull

Yet, when the mist lifts and sea and sky divorce
Beauty blunts the edge of reason
As couples lie beside the flowering gorse
And once more kissing is in season